4/06

Harlem Photographs 1932–1940

Aaron Siskind

Foreword

Gordon Parks

Harlem: A Document

Maricia Battle

Text From Federal Writers' Project

Edited by Ann Banks

National Museum of American Art

Smithsonian Institution Press

Washington and London

The publication of *Harlem: Photographs by Aaron Siskind, 1932–1940*
accompanies an exhibition of the photographs organized by the
National Museum of American Art, Smithsonian Institution, Merry A. Foresta, curator.
Exhibition dates: November 22, 1990–March 17, 1991.

Harlem: Photographs by Aaron Siskind, 1932–1940 was originally published as
Harlem Document: Photographs 1932–1940.

Design: Malcolm Grear

ISBN: 1-56098-041-9

LC Number: 90-63168

Foreword

Aaron Siskind's Harlem document, a mirror of my own past, speaks explicitly for itself. It is an ongoing memory of Black people living in crowded kitchenettes; suffering the loneliness of rented bedrooms; praying in leftover churches, and grasping a patch of happiness whenever and wherever they could find it. It is a nostalgic look at a kind of past that threatens to hang around Harlem for a long time to come—to doom it to further frustration and unrest. Those same tenements that once imprisoned me are still there, refusing to crumble, holding other restless black boys for sentence without trial.

I remember swarms of slow-moving people, moving close together up on Lenox Avenue—past the chili shacks, rib joints, funeral parlors and storefront churches—knowing one another but seldom bothering to speak. A city of blackness crammed inside a white city where, when you walked out the door, you became a stranger.

"Shake it to the east.
 Shake it to the west.
 Shake it at the one
 You like the best."

And a lot of them found strength to "shake that thing" after a hard day of work. In the evenings they gave in to whatever their bodies wanted and, without shame, broke into laughter, song and dance to kill the memories of the day; to keep alive what little hope there was left; and to help fill those empty spots in their souls.

"Good morning blues.
 Blues how do you do?"

And people expressed their feelings with the blues, those sad songs that cried and laughed at the same time. And white people from downtown came to eat black food and let their feet dance to black Music at the *Cotton Club*—where black people couldn't eat or dance. They don't get away with that anymore up there. Harlem's new worldliness no longer puts up with that kind of thing.

But now, like then, the older folks still go to church on Sundays; still manage, through song and prayer, to get strength from their faith. Church is still the eternal spring of hope, the main road to the heavenly kingdom. It is only there that they are wholly themselves. So, with their nickels and dimes they keep the little Bethels, Pilgrims, Good Hopes, White Rocks and Mount Olives going. They are still God's children. But while they lean on him, their own children take to the streets, bars and junky pads—sometimes winding up in jail. Sometimes in the morgue.

Harlem has meant a lot of things to a lot of people. For me, in those days, it meant hunger, cultural devastation, unrequited longing and disillusionment. To others it was the swinging, exciting capitol of the entire Black world, the exotic mecca of melting music, good times and dancing feet. Yet, for some, it was a sanctuary where loftier dreams were fostered; where now and then some of those dreams were realized, but where mostly they were hopelessly spent. To just about everyone who has worked in the vital processes of its survival, whose life has been textured by its tradition, Harlem is a place that won't give up. Wobbly now under the impact of the past decades, its history mirrors those problems its mother country once endured. What it needs, what it wants, what it still struggles for is what America finally became.

"Heh, baby, how you doing?" That was a familiar greeting when I was a young man up in Harlem. Today it's, "What's happening, brother? What's shaking up and down the line?"

Well, there are a few new buildings up there now, looking smugly down upon all the old ones. And some blacks, who once turned their backs on the place, are going back to try it again. Good music, prayer and laughter is still in the air—and so are the songs of the fish peddler and watermelon man. Joy, sorrow, happiness and despair still hang out together, and jobless young people with anger in their eyes, stand on the corners and stare into space. "Nothing's happening," they say. " Nothing's shaking *up* or *down* the line."

GORDON PARKS

Harlem: A Document

The images in this book are from three different Harlem projects begun by Aaron Siskind during the 1930s. The earliest of these informal, open-ended series dates from after Siskind joined the Photo League in 1932, others were made during his participation with the League's Feature Group, and some are from the "Most Crowded Block" project of 1939, 1940. At various times in the ensuing years they have been grouped under the title "Harlem Document," in part because Siskind was so instrumental in organizing that project at the League, in part because that heading so succinctly describes the purpose of all the images.

Originally published in 1981, the reprinting of this book allows us the opportunity to once again explore Siskind's Harlem, and also to re-examine a documentary style of photography that can be as subjective as it is descriptive. Envisioned by Siskind in 1940, now with text from stories collected by Federal Writers Frank Byrd, Dorothy West, Vivian Morris, and Ralph Ellison, the present book serves as one picture of Harlem. It is a book which, in Siskind's words, "image and text [melt] together...and become more expressive than many words."

What the "Harlem Document" was intended to be probably never can be accurately answered. In 1937, approximately eight photographers, including Aaron Siskind, were involved in a project known as the "Harlem Document." The project was designed to culminate in a book that looked at the diverse aspects of the Harlem community. It was a collaboration between Michael Carter, an African-American sociologist and editor of the League's house organ, *Photo Notes*, and the group of eight photographers. Carter's responsibility was to provide the text to accompany the photographers' pictures. Besides Siskind, who was project director, the other photographers were Harold Corsini, Lucy Ashjian, Beatrice Kosofshy, Richard Lyon, Jack Mendelson (Manning), Sol Prom (Fabricant), and Morris Engle. Carter met with the group for two years, providing background information and statistics. He also introduced the photographers to Harlem leaders and residents. The book was never published and Carter's manuscript disappeared.

The photographic "Harlem Document," however, was completed in 1940. The "document" only portrayed that portion of the Harlem community of interest to the Photo League. Forty pictures were exhibited widely throughout Harlem in 1939 and were included in the San Francisco World's Fair in 1940. Some of the pictures were published in *Fortune* (July 1939) and in *Look* (May 1940) with captions prepared by Carter. Prior to the publication of the Siskind book (1981) and since, the other images from the "Harlem Document" have not been seen or exhibited. Some of the images but not the entire body of work were seen in the "Photographic Crossroads: The Photo League" exhibition that traveled in the United States and Canada in 1978. The 1981 book, originally published as *Harlem Document: Photographs 1932–1940*, represents a selection of some of the pictures made for the Photo League project by Aaron Siskind.

The New York Photo League, which began life as the New York Worker's Film and Photo League in 1929, was an organization composed of professional and amateur photographers committed to using documentary photography to effect social reforms. There were two factions active in the first League, those dedicated to the original goals of documenting social conditions for the purpose of reform and those desiring to address aesthetic issues and explore different forms.[1] These factions split and in 1936 formed three separate entities — the New York Film and Photo League, Frontier Films, and the (New York) Photo League. Those members intent on embracing aesthetic concerns were part of the latter two groups.

An article published in the August 1938 issue of *Photo Notes*, the newsletter of the Photo League, expressed the League's philosophy: "Photography has tremendous social value. Upon the photographer rests the responsibility and duty of recording a true image of the world as it is today. Moreover, he must not only show us how we live, but indicate the logical development of our lives."

Opposed to the "stultifying influence of the pictorialists" the article declared that "the Photo League's task is to put the camera back into the hands of honest photographers, who will use it to photograph America. We must include within our ranks the thousands of New York's amateurs. We must include the established workers who have creative desires and who do not find an adequate outlet in their day-to-day tasks...."

Further reorganization in 1936 led to the formation of the Feature Group by Aaron Siskind within the League. The Feature Group was a special documentary production unit that led the League in projects for a decade. Its quality productions and longevity were due primarily to the perseverance of Siskind who functioned as leader, mentor, and producing member. Its other members were mostly younger, serious amateur photographers. From 1936 to 1940, Siskind and this group investigated the photo documentary essay form that was then being used by the Farm Security Administration (FSA) photographers and *Life* magazine. Without funding for the unit, the only motivation for Siskind's group was to document the effects of the Depression. Siskind demanded that the group assume control of the medium through technical proficiency, while simultaneously producing features that exposed existing social conditions.

The "Harlem Document" was the best known and most successful production of the Feature Group. The quality of the "Harlem Document" images was due primarily to the personal interest and guidance provided by Siskind. His insistence that the photographers master the medium and thoroughly understand its limitations and possibilities resulted in final images that addressed both social and aesthetic concerns.

Aaron Siskind's interest in photography developed after his experiences with both music and poetry when he was an English teacher in the New York public school system. His early pictures were said to have been attempts at transferring musical and poetic concepts into images.[2] Later, as a young adult, Siskind did everything from making political speeches on soapboxes in Manhattan to becoming a member of the Junior Young People's Socialist League (YPSL).[3]

A friend gave Siskind his first camera in 1930. He soon discovered his attraction for the instrument, and almost simultaneously he discovered and joined the Photo League. At the League he found people who shared his political and social concerns and who were capable and willing to discuss technical information about photography. Many of the members were children of Jewish immigrants and most, like Siskind, were well educated. Their exhibited images documented illiteracy, discrimination, and poverty and called for social reforms on behalf of the working classes. Before joining the League, Siskind had already photo-graphed some of the poverty-stricken areas of Manhattan and was searching for reaction and criticism to these pictures. The Photo League offered him a natural platform to discuss his work and receive that criticism. Impressed by the work of other League members he was motivated to produce similar documents. It was his entry into the world of photography.

As a photographer Siskind explored symbols and metaphors to create a visual relationship that balanced aesthetic concerns with social documents. Throughout his career the contrast of subject and symbol have dominated. In a June 1945 article published in *Minicam Photography*, titled "The Drama of Objects," Siskind described his approach to documentary photographs:

...Producing a photographic document involves preparation in excess. There is first the examination of the idea of the project. Then the visits to the scene, the casual conversations, and more formal interviews—talking, and listening, and looking, looking. You read what's been written, and dig out facts and figures for your own writing. Follows the discussions to arrive at a point of view and its crystallization into a statement of aim. And finally, the pictures themselves, each one planned, talked, taken, and examined in terms of the whole. I worked pretty much this way in making "Harlem Document." However, I cautioned my co-workers on this job to become as passive as possible when they faced the subject, to de-energize for the moment their knowledge of the ideas about the subject, to let the facts fall away and at that crucial moment to permit the subject to speak for itself and in its own way....

It was with these concerns in mind that Siskind created the images of Harlem. He photographed Harlem with a large format camera and tripod. Although he tried not to invade their privacy, his subjects were acutely aware of his presence. In some of the images, however, you can sense from a subject's reaction an unintended intrusion. There are exceptions: pictures where direct confrontation occurs between Siskind and his sitter or where Siskind directly met the returned look of his subject. Most of the images showing this confrontation are from "The Most Crowded Block in the World," a project Siskind worked on with Max Yavno and Michael Carter but never completed. After Carter, Yavno and Siskind left the League, and Siskind went on to make 150 images on this one square block in Harlem. It was intended to be an extension of the "Harlem Document," but Yavno was drafted in 1941 and Carter simply disappeared with no explanation at about the same time. Some of these pictures are included in *Harlem*.

With his work in Harlem Siskind's style may have been changing. "In working from the documentary approach, I had always tried to find what kind of meaning you could get in a picture of that kind, and was beginning to feel that I was not getting it. I felt I wasn't getting anything really personal, really powerful and special....My documentary pictures were very quiet and very formal."[4]

Since 1940 Siskind's style and the types of images he produces has changed. Though Aaron Siskind has never looked back to the time when he created the "Harlem Document," we are grateful that he provided us with these and related photographs. They were created by an artist with only the best of intentions: to make a nation aware of its economic injustice and to hope for social reform. Ultimately, however, the photographs better proclaimed the aesthetic priorities of an artist who sought control over his medium. They were not to be insensitive intrusions into the life of a community but, rather, compelling pieces of art to probe the social and aesthetic perceptions of the artist.

MARICIA BATTLE

NOTES

1 Anne Tucker, "The Photo League," *Ovo Magazine* 10, no. 40/41 (1981): 4.

2 Carl Chiarenza, *Aaron Siskind: Pleasures and Terrors* (Little, Brown and Co.), 6.

3 Carl Chiarenza, "Form and Content in the Early Work of Aaron Siskind," *The Massachusetts Review* 19:4 (Winter 1978): 810.

4 Jaromir Stephany unpublished interview with Aaron Siskind, February 1963. This interview is in the private papers of Jaromir Stephany.

Introduction

On a spring evening in 1939 Ralph Ellison sat in Eddie's Bar on St. Nicholas Avenue and took notes as a Pullman porter just off work lamented his move north to Harlem. "I'm in New York," he said, "but New York ain't in me." The porter Ellison listened to was one of nine people then living in Harlem—including a jazz drummer, a street-corner orator, a rent party proprietress, a prostitute, a "conjure man," a show girl and a peddler of fish and vegetables—whose stories are published here. They were among thousands of first-person narratives (what are now called "oral history") collected during the last years of the Great Depression by members of the Federal Writers' Project.

The Project was based on the idea that unemployed writers had as much right to jobs as unemployed carpenters. With its companion federal arts projects—music, art, and theater—the Writers' Project was part of the New Deal's national work relief program, the Works Progress Administration (WPA) during Franklin Roosevelt's presidency. At its peak the Federal Writers' Project employed about 6500 writers for about $20. a week. Of the considerable number who went on to achieve national reputations, some were among the most talented black writers in America. Novelists Ralph Ellison, Margaret Walker, Zora Neale Hurston, Arna Bontemps, Frank Yerby and Richard Wright all served apprenticeships on the Writers' Project. It was to young black writers that the opportunity was particularly important; they had virtually no other hope of work. Working on the Writers' Project encouraged Ralph Ellison to think of himself for the first time as a professional. "Actually to be *paid* for writing," he recalls, "why that was a wonderful thing."

The stories published here were collected by Federal Writers Frank Byrd, Dorothy West, and Vivian Morris as well as Ellison. Because they were black and themselves "on relief," they were accepted as sympathetic equals by those they talked with. Frank Byrd recalls how he made friends with some of the Harlem residents he interviewed: "I was a neighborhood boy. I played handball, I played basketball, I played stickball and all the rest of the stuff in the neighborhood. That way you got to know the people. And that was the beginning, you see . . . Then you had to pass the time of day with them until you reached the point where you felt a warm relationship so that you could talk, so that *they* could talk.

Ralph Ellison also favored an informal method of finding people to interview. "I hung around playgrounds. I hung around the streets, the bars. I went into hundreds of apartment buildings and just knocked on doors. I would tell some stories to get people going and then I'd sit back and try to get it down as accurately as I could."

In rendering such first-person narratives, Ellison began to experiment with ways of capturing the sound of their speech which he later refined in his novel *Invisible Man*. Instead of using misspellings to convey the dialect he heard on the Harlem streets, he developed a technique of transcribing that approximated the idiom. "I tried to use my ear for dialogue to give an impression of just how people sounded." And the stories they told taught him about his own history. He says, "Once you touched the history of the blacks in New York, you were deep into American history."

The Harlem that Ellison and other Federal Writers chronicled in 1939 had become a painful place. This nerve center of black America had been created during the years surrounding World War I by large migrations of Southern blacks. They had come to fill jobs created by industrial expansion and left open to them because war had reduced European immigration. In the 1920s Harlem began to blossom in a vibrant new urban culture, a rising standard of living and a growing sense of self-respect. But the Depression smashed these gains and by 1937 the unemployment rate for blacks was at least three times that of whites. Times were so hard that whites took jobs they would not have considered before the crash, leaving blacks out of work and bitter.

Some of the people whose stories are collected here vent their bitterness—toward local merchants who did not hire blacks for any but the most menial jobs; toward whites who came "slumming" up to Harlem to hear jazz and find black prostitutes.

Others put their faith in magic—in conjurers' spells for when "your luck goes back on you"—or in divine justice to come —"God's time when everybody'll be equal." Still others describe how they survived by combining enterprise and entertainment— in hawking fish, in throwing rent parties.

The men and women of Harlem who talked to the Federal Writers had in common a vividly expressive verbal style. Their stories have an immediacy and a vitality that continues to make itself felt across the span of more than forty years. The rich oral tradition of black America, the gift for drawing poetry from the everyday round of work or play, was expressed by Clyde "Kingfish" Smith when he was asked about the source of inspiration for his original fish songs: "On the street whatever comes to my mind I say it if I think it will be good . . . It's got to be more an expression than a routine."

ANN BANKS

Harlem   *Interviews*

Acknowledgments

I would like to thank Knute Walker for
sharing his thoughts on Harlem and the
Federal Writers' Project.

A.B.

I started singing when I started peddling; that was in 1932. "Heigho fish man, bring down your dishpan," that's what started it. "Fish ain't but five cents a pound." It was hard times then—the depression and people can hardly believe fish is five cents a pound, so they started buying. There were quite a few peddlers and somebody has to have something extra to attract attention. So when I came around, started making a rhyme, it was a hit right away. One of the first things I learned about peddling was to be any success at all, you had to have an original cry. I know several peddlers that started out and they hollered, Old Fish Man, but it doesn't work.

I've gone blocks where several fish men have gone already and sold fish like nobody had been there. When I sing, a certain amount of people will be standing around, looking and listening, and that attracts more people. Whenever people see a crowd they think it's a bargain so they want to get in on it. When I sing it will be so loud that people come to the windows and look out. They come down with bedroom shoes on, with bathrobes, and some have pans or newspapers to put the fish in.

When I first come to a block nobody pays any attention. Then I start singing, get them to laughing and looking and soon they start buying. A lot of them just hang around to hear the song. I always try to give the best fish I can for the money and that makes repeated customers. A lot of people wait for my individual cry. The average day I cover about eight blocks and spend about an hour in each block, sometimes longer.

When I have crabs the kids like to see the crabs jump and bite, so they stand around in big crowds. Sometimes, when I sing, the kids be dancing the Lindy Hop and Trucking. Women buy most of the fish. I find Home Relief and WPA people the best customers. They buy more. They have to budget more near than the average family.

In white and Jewish neighborhoods I feature the words but in the colored neighborhood I feature the tune. In the Jewish neighborhood they appreciate the rhyming and the words more, while in the colored neighborhood they appreciate the swinging and the tune, as well as the words. I put in a sort of jumping rhythm for the colored folks. That swing music comes right from old colored folks spirituals.

I say whatever comes to my mind if I think it will be good. The main idea is when I got something I want to put over I just find something to rhyme with it. And the main requirement for that is mood. You gotta be in the mood. You got to put yourself in it. You've got to feel it. It's got to be more an expression than a routine. Of course sometimes a drink of King Kong helps.

A song like this I'd just look on the wagon and rhyme up something to match with it. When I sang this song, this morning, I was just thinking of something to rhyme then.

I got vegetables today,
So don't go away.
Stick around
And you'll hear me say,
Buy 'em by the pound,
Put em in a sack
Hurry up and get 'em
Cause I'm not coming back.
I got apples, onions and collard greens.
I got the best string beans,
That I ever seen
I got oranges, tomatoes, nice southern
   sweet potatoes.
I got yellow yams
From Birmingham.
And if you want some,
Here I come
And if you don't want none
I don't give a
Yam, yam, yam
I got green greens
From New Orleans.
I got the greenest greens
I ever seen,
And I sure seen
A whole lot of greens
I got cauliflower
And mustard greens.
The best cauliflower
I ever seen.
So buy some,
Try some,
Take 'em home and fry some.

———

645 OUR OWN COMMUNITY 645
GROCERY & DELICATESSEN
645 GROCERY - DELICATESSEN 645
MILK 6
SUGAR 5 lbs. 22
BACON 10
STARCH 8
DOG FOOD 3 13
5¢ 5¢
Pepsi-Cola

This was my first original fish song. I put words from this into some of the others. This was the first fish song in my own tune. So after the people begin to get too familiar with the tune, I grasped the idea of changing my tune to get the tune of the most popular song hit of that time.

> *Yo, ho, ho,* fish man!
> Bring down your dish pan!
> Fish ain't but five cents a pound.
> So come on down,
> And gather around,
> I got the best fish
> That's in this town.
> I got porgies,
> Crockers too.
> I ain't got but a few,
> So you know what to do.
> Come on down,
> And gather round,
> Cause my fish ain't
> But five cents a pound.
> I've got 'em large
> And I've got 'em small;
> I got 'em long and I got 'em tall,
> I've got 'em fried,
> I got 'em broiled,
> And I can't go home 'till I sell 'em all!
> So yo, ho, ho, fish man!
> Bring down your dish pan!
> Cause fish ain't but five cents a pound!

———

> I can't go home 'till all my fish is gone.
> Stormy weather.
> I can't keep my fish together,
> Sellin 'em all the time.
> If you don't buy 'em
> Old rag man will get me.
> If you do buy 'em
> You folks 'll kinda let me
> Walk in the sun once more.
> I don't see why
> You folks don't come and buy
> Stormy weather,
> Come,
> Let's get together,
> Sellin 'em all the time.

I wouldn't sing this one in a Jewish neighborhood. They don't know the tune and they couldn't appreciate that song. Only in a colored neighborhood.

———

Say, ice man,
I want some today.
So hurry up and bring it,
Before I go away.
Bring fifty pound,
And hurry right down,
Cause you got
The best ice in this town.
You can chop it up
And make it small,
Better bring it quick
Or not at all.
I want to put it on my fish
Because it's nice and hot,
And I better do something
Before they rot.

———

I've got crabs.
They bite and nab.
I got crabs,
That punch and jab.
I got crabs,
That sing like Cab.
So be like my cousin,
And buy a couple of dozen,
Of my crabs today.
Buy 'em by the dozen.
I'll put 'em in a sack,
Hurry up and get 'em
Cause I ain't coming back.
Come on folks
I got crabs today.
Better get some,
Before I go away,
Cause all my crabs
Are nice and live,
You can take my word
That that's no jive.

———

Jim, jam, jump, jumpin jive
Make you buy yo fish on the east side,
Oh, boy,
What you gonna say there cats?
Jim, jam, jump, jumpin jive.
When you eat my fish,
You'll eat four or five.
Pal of mine, pal of mine, swanee shore.
Come on, buy my fish once more.
Oh, boy, oh boy,
Jim, jam, jump, jumpin jive.
Make you dig your fish on the
   mellow side.
Oh boy, what you gonna say there cats?
Don't you hear them hep cats call?
Come on, boys, and let's buy 'em all.
Oh boy, what you gonna say there cats?

Jump joints: that means where they dance and drink and smoke the marijuana weeds. The marijuana weed is a jumping jive. The expression is knock me a jive there. That means, give me a marijuana cigarette. When you have the jumping jive on, you're supposed to do all these things and buy the fish.

———

B   *Children's Street Rhymes*

Once upon a time
Goose drink wine
Monkey did the Shimmy on the
    trolly car line
trolly car broke
monkey choke
and they all went to heaven
    in an old tin boat.

———

Hello Bill
Where you going Bill
Downtown Bill
What for Bill
To pay my gas bill
How much Bill
Ten dollar bill
Good bye Bill.

———

Hey Mister, If you shut up in an iron house
without any windows and you didn't have
nothing but a baseball bat?
In an Iron house?
Yeah, yeah that's right. Come on mister,
what'll you do?
Well, I guess I don't know.
Gee, don't you know how to play baseball?
Anybody who can play baseball knows
how to get outa there.
Well how would I get out?
Three strikes and you out, Mister . . .
You see what he means.

    THREE STRIKES AN YOU OUT!

———

Little Sallie Water,
Sitting in the Saucer.
Rise, Sallie, rise
Wipe your winking eyes.
Turn to the east, my darling,
Turn to the west, my darling,
Turn to the very one that you
    love the best.
Put your hands on your hips
and let your backbone shake my darling
Shake it to the east, my darling,
Shake it to the west, my darling,
Shake it to the very one that you
    love the best.

———

Once upon a time
Goose drink wine
Monkey did the Shimmy on the
    trolly car line
trolly car broke
monkey choke
and they all went to heaven
    in an old tin boat.

———

Can you read
Can you write
Can you smoke your daddy's pipe?

———

Gypsy gypsy live in a tent
she couldn't afford to pay her rent
she borrowed once
she borrowed twice
She passed it over to you

———

Joe Louis
Don't catch me
Catch that man behind the tree
he stole apples
I stole none
Put him in jail just for fun

———

Chicken in the car
Car wouldn't go
Chicken jump out
The car went slow.

———

I been doin this for goin on two years now, hoping an wishing that some day I'll get a break and be somebody. I want to see my name in electric lights an in all the newspapers.—I knows I'm black, an I knows black folks has gotta go a long ways before they arrive. But I got one thing in the back a this head a mine, an that is: "Color Can't Conquer Courage." I'm gonna be like Florence Mills. . . . Does you remember her, Miss? Y'knows when she started dancin she was only 5 years old? At an entertainment her Sunday School was puttin on it was, and she kept on from there to the nickelodeons on 135th Street an on, an on, til she became the sensation of two continents. She danced and sang for kings, princes and all the rest a royalty. Lawd, am I hopin that one a these nights some a them white folks who come to Harlem lookin for talent will see something in me an give me a chance where I wouldn't have t'do four shows a day for seven days a week.

Florence Mills knocked em dead every time. The Duke of Windsor—then he was the Prince of Wales—saw her strut her stuff thirteen times. They even called her the Negro Ambassador to the World, but things like that never went to her head.

And did she have pride in her own people! Whenever she was playin in a show on Broadway she always saw to it that it come to Harlem even for a week so that her own people who didn't have money enough to go down on Broadway would not be denied the privilege of seein her. Lawd, I can hear her now, singin: "I'm a little Blackbird lookin' for a Bluebird," her feet dancin as though she had electric sparks goin through her body. She sure did her stuff with enjoyment. I'm gonna be that someday shore enough. I'm 23 now. Keep watchin the newspapers—you gonna read about me. Florence Mills was one a God's chosen chillren. She make as much as three thousand five hundred dollars a week an she didn't leave 133rd Street either, until God saw fit to take her off this wicked earth. Sometime I think God ain't fair as He should be. Florence Mills die when she reached the top. She didn't enjoy the money she made. She was in demand. They had big plans for her an all of a sudden God came on the scene. She was one of His chillren; He step right in an clip her wings. She was a God-given Genius. People like Florence Mills make this world a better place to live in. She did a helluva lot to wipe out race prejudice. If all they say about the Hereafter is true, then the Heavenly Gates must a swung ajar for Florence Mills to enter an Shine in Heaven, cause she sure did shine down here. That was some year and month of disappointments in Harlem, November 1927. The Republicans swept Harlem, Marcus Garvey was bein deported an our Queen a Happiness died.

I was sitting up on the bandstand drumming, trying to make myself some beat-up change. Wasn't such a crowd in the place that night, just a bunch a them beer-drinkers. I was looking down at em dancing and wishing that things would liven up. Then a man come up and give me *four* dollars just to sing one number. Well, I was singing for that man. I was really laying it Jack, just like Marian Anderson. What the hell are you talking about; I'd sing all night after that cat done give me four bucks; thats almost a fin! But this is what brings you down. One a these bums come up to the stand and says to the banjo player:

"If you monkeys don't play some music, I'm gonna throw you outta de jernt."

Man, I quit singing and looked at that sonofabitch. Then I got mad. I said:

"Where the goddam hell you come from, you gonna throw somebody *outa* this band? How you get so bad? Why you poor Brooklyn motherfriger, I'll wreck this goddam place with you."

Man, he looked at me. I said:

"Don't look at me goddamit, I mean what I say!"

By this time everybody is standing around listening. I said:

"I oughta snatch your goddam head off. Oh, I know the rest'll try to gang me. But they won't get me before I get to you. You crummy bastard."

Then man, I make a break for my pocket, like I was pulling my gun. Ha, Ha, goddam! You oughta seen em fall back from this cat. This bum had on glasses and you oughta seen him holding up his hands and gitting outa my way. Then the boss come up running and put the sonofabitch out into the street and told me to get back to work. Hell, I scaired the hell out of that bastard. A poor sonofabitch! Drinking beer and coming up talking to us like that! You see he thought cause we was black he could talk like he wanted to. In a night club and drinking beer! I fixed him. I bet he won't try that no more.

Man, a poor white man is a bringdown. He ain't got nothing. He can't get nothing. And he thinks cause he's white he's got to impress you cause you black.

Then some of em comes up and try to be your friend. Like the other night, I'm up on the stand drumming and singing, trying to make myself some change. I was worried. I got a big old boy, dam near big as me, and every time I look up he's got to have something. Well, the other night I hadn't made a dam thing. And I was sitting there drumming when one of these bums what hangs around the place, one a these slap-happy jitterbugs, comes up to me and says:

"You stink!"

Now you know that made me mad before I even knowed what he was talking about. A white cat coming up to me talking about I stink! I said: "What you talking about. What you mean I stink? He said: "You ain't a good fellow like the other cats. You won't take me up to Harlem and show me around." I said:

"Hell yes, mammydoger, I stink! If that's what you mean I'm gon always stink. You'll never catch me carrying a bunch of you poor sonsabitches up there. What the hell you gonna do when you get up there? You ain't got nothing. Hell, you poor as I am. I don't see you coming down to Harlem to carry me up to show me the Bronx. You dam right I stink." Man, he just looks at me now and says:

"Jack, you sho a funny cat."

Can you beat that? He oughta know I ain't got no use for him. DAM!

Another one comes up to me—another one a these beer-drinking bums—and says:

"I want to go up to your house some-time."

I said:

"Fo what! Now you tell me fo what!" I said: What-in-the-world do you want to come up to *my* place for? You ain't got nothing and I sho ain't got nothing. What's a poor colored cat and a poor white cat gonna do together? You ain't got nothing cause you too dumb to get it. And I ain't got nothins cause I'm black. I guess you got your little ol skin, that's the reason? I'm sup-posed to feel good cause you walk in my house and sit in my chairs? Hell, that skin ain't no more good to you than mine is to me. You cain't marry one a DuPont's daughters, and I know dam well I cain't. So what the hell you gon do to my place?"

Aw man, I have to get these white cats told. They think you supposed to feel good cause they friendly to you. Boy I don't fool with em. They just the reason why I caint get ahead now. They try to get all a man's money. That's just the reason why I found me a place up the street here. Got two rooms in a private house with a private bath. These other cats go down to Ludwig Bauman's* and give him all their money so they can meet you on the street and say: "Oh you *must* come up to my apartment sometimes. Oh yes, yes, I have some lovely furniture. You just must come up some-time; You know, man, they want to show off. But me I done got wise. I'm getting my stuff outa junk shops, second hand stores, anywhere, I ain't giving these Jews my money. Like the chicks. I used to get my check and go out with the boys and pick up some of these fine feathered chicks. You know the light chicks with the fine hair. We'd go out making all the gin mills, buy-ing liquor. I'd take em to a room and have a ball. Then I'd wake up in the morning with all my beat-up change gone and I'd have to face my wife and tell her some deep lie that she didn't believe. I don't do that no more. Now I give most of my money to my wife. And I put the rest on the numbers. And when I see the fine chicks I tell em they have to wait till the numbers jumps out.

See this bag? I got me a head a cabbage and two ears a corn. I'm going up here and get me a side a bacon. When I get home, gonna cook the cabbage and bacon, gonna make me some corn fritters and set back in

---

*A furniture store on 125th St.

my twenty-five-dollars-a-month room and eat my fritters and cabbage and tell the Jews to forgit it! Jack I'm just sitting back waiting, cause soon things is gonna narrow down to the fine point. Hitler's gonna reach in a few months and grab and then things'll start. All the white folks'll be killing off one another. And I hope they do a good job! Then there won't be nobody left but Sam. Then we'll be fighting it out among ourselves. That'll be a funky fight. Aw hell yes! When Negroes start running things I think I'll have to get off the earth before it's too late!

I'm in New York, but New York ain't in me. You understand? I'm in New York, but New York ain't in me. What do I mean? Listen. I'm from Jacksonville Florida. Been in New York twenty-five years. I'm a New Yorker! But I'm in New York and New York ain't in me. Yuh understand? Naw, naw, you don't get me. What do they do. Take Lenox Avenue. Take Seventh Avenue. Take Sugar Hill! Pimps. Numbers. Cheating these poor people outa what they got. Shooting, cutting, backbiting, all them things. Yuh see? Yuh see what I mean? *I'M* in New York, but *New York ain't* in me! Don't laugh, don't laugh. I'm laughing but I don't mean it; it ain't funny. Yuh see. I'm on Sugar Hill, but Sugar Hill ain't on me.

I come here twenty-five years ago. Bright lights. Pretty women. More space to move around. Son, if I had-a got New York in me I'd a-been dead a long time ago. What happened the other night. Yuh heard about the shooting up here in the hill. Take that boy. I knowed him! Anybody been around this hill knows him, n they know he went to a bad man. What'd he do? Now mind yuh now, his brother's a big-shot. Makes plenty money. Got a big car an a fine office. But *he* comes up on this hill tearin up people's property if they don't pay him protection. Last night he walks into this wop's place up the street n tries to tear it up. Now yuh know that's a bad man, gonna tear up the wop's place. Well, he stepped out the door

n a bunch of them wops showed up in a car n tried to blow him away. *He* had too much New York. I'm in New York, yuh see? But New York ain't in me! Hell yes, he went and got too much New York, yuh understand what I tryin to tell yuh?

I been in New York twenty-five years! But I ain't never bothered nobody. Ain't never done nothin to nobody. I ain't no bad fellow. Shore I drink. I like good whiskey. I drinks but I ain't drunk. Yuh think I'm drunk. I don't *talk* drunk do I? I drinking n I got money in mah pockets. But I ain't throwing ma money away. Hell, I talking sense, ain't I. Yuh heard me way in yonder didn't yuh? Yuh came to me, heard me. I didn't have to come after yuh did I? If I hada been talking foolishness yuh wouldn't a paid me no mind. Hell, I know I'm right. I got something to say. I got something to say n I ain't no preacher neither. I'm drinking. I likes to drink. It's good for mah stomach. *Good* whiskey's good for anybody's stomach. Look at the bottle. Mount Vernon! Good Whiskey. What did the saint say? He said a little spirits is good for the stomach, good to warm the spirit. Now where did that come from? Yuh don't know, yuh too young. Yuh young Negroes don't know the Bible. Don't laugh, don't laugh. Look here, I'll tell you somethin:

Some folks drinks to cut the fool,
But some folks drinks to think
I drinks to think.

It's too bad about them two submarines. They can experiment an everything, but they cain't go but so far. Then God steps in. Them fellows is trying to make some think what'll stay down. They said they'd done it, but look what happened. Take back in 1912. They built a ship called the Titanic. Think they built it over in England;* I think that was where it was built. Anyway, they said it couldn't sink. It was for all the big rich folks: John Jacob Astor —all the big aristocrats. Nothing the color of this could git on the boat. Naw suh! Didn't want nothing look like me on it. One girl went down to go with her madam and they told her she couldn't go. They didn't want nothing look like this on there. They told the madam, "You can go, but she cain't." The girl's madam got mad and told em if the girl didn't go she wasn't going. And she didn't neither. Yessuh, she stayed right here.

Well, they got this big boat on the way over to England. They said she couldn't sink—that was man talking. It was so big they tell me that was elevators in it like across yonder in that building. Had the richest folks in the world on it just having a big tune. Got over near England, almost ready to dock, and ups an hits an iceberg, and sank! That was the boat they said was so big it couldn't sink. They didn't want nothing look like this on it; no sir! And

---

*The Titanic was sailing toward the United States when it sank.

don't you think that woman wasn't glad she stuck by that girl. She was plenty glad. Man can go only so far. Then God steps in. Sho, they can experiment around. They can do a heap. They can even make a man. But they caint make him breathe. Why the other day I was down on 125th St. and 8th Ave. They got one of them malted milk places. Well, suh, they got a cow on the counter. It looks like a real cow. Got hair. I was standing there looking and the doggone thing moved its head and wagged its tail; man done even made a cow. But, they had to do it with electricity.

God's the only one can give life. God made all this, and he made it for everybody. And he made it equal. This breeze and these green leaves out here is for everybody. The same sun's shining down on everybody. This breeze comes from God and man caint do nothing about it. I breathe the same air old man Ford and old man Rockefeller breathe. They got all the money and I ain't got nothing, but they got to breathe the same air I do.

Man cain't make no man. Less see now: This heahs nineteen-hundred-and-twenty-nine.* For 1900 years man's had things his way. He's been running the world to suit hisself. It's just like your father owned that building over there and told you you could live in it if you didn't do certain things. And then you did what he told you not to. And he finds out and says, "Go on, you can have

_____
*It was 1939.

the whole building, I won't have nothing else to do with it. You can turn it upside-down if you want to." Well, that was the way it was in the world. Adam and Eve sinned in the Garden and God left the world to itself. Men been running it like they want to. They been running it like they want to for 1900 years. Rich folks done took all the land. They got all the money. Men down to the City Hall making $50,000 a year and nothing like this cain't even scrub the marble floors or polish the brass what they got down there. Old man Ford and J. P. Morgan got all the money and folks in this part cain't even get on relief. But you just watch: the Lawd made all men equal and pretty soon now it's gonna be that way again. I'm a man. I breathe the same air old man Ford breathes cause God made man equal. God formed man in his own image. He made Adam out of the earth; not like this concrete we sitting on, but out of dirt, clay. Like you seen a kid making a snowman. He'll git him a stick and make the arms. And he'll git another stick and make for his neck; and so on, just like we got bones. That was the way God made man. Made him outa clay and in his own image: That was the way he made Adam. One drop of God's blood made all the nations in the world; Africans, Germans, Chinamen, Jews, Indians; all come from one drop of God's blood. God took something outa Adam and made woman, he made Eve. The preachers tell a lie and say it was his rib. But they have to lie, I guess. They didn't do nothing but sit

back in the shed and let you do all the work anyway. But God went into Adam and took something out and made Eve. That's the Scriptures; it said he took *something*. I caint remember the exact words, but it said he took *something* and it didn't say nothing bout no rib. Eve started having children. Some of em was black and some of em was white. But they was all equal. God didn't know no color; we all the same. All he want from man is this heart thumping the blood. Them what take advantage of skin like this got to come by God. They gonna pay.

They tell me bout George Washington. He was the first president this country ever had. First thing I heard was he said keep us look like this down in the cornfield. He tole em "Don't let em have no guns. You ain't to let em have no knife. Don't let em have nothing." He tole em if they wanted to have a strong nation to keep us down. He said if ever they git guns in they hands they'll rise up and take the land; don't let em have nothing. But he didn't say nothing bout no pick and ax!

They been carrying out what he said. God didn't say nothing. That was just man's idea and here in this country they been carrying out what old man George Washington said. But God's time is coming. Today you hear all these folks got millions of dollars talking bout God. They ain't fooling nobody, though. They even got "IN GOD WE TRUST" on all the silver money. But it don't mean nothing. This sun and air is

God's. It don't belong to nobody and caint no few get it all to theyself. People around this park can have all they want. But you wait. God's gonna straighten it all out. Look at the dust blowing in the wind. That's the way all the money they got gonna be. You see things, folks, they call white, but man ain't got no idea of how white God gon make things. Money won't be worth no more'n that dust blowing on the ground. Won't be no men down to Washington ~~making fifty thousand dollars a week and~~ folks cain't hardly make eighteen dollars a month. Everybody'll be equal, in God's time. Won't be no old man Rockefeller, no suh! Today you cain't even buy a job if you had the money to do it with. Won't be nothing like that then. He'll let loose and something'll slip down here and them what done took advantage of everything'll be floating down the river. You'll go over to the North River, and over to the East River and you'll see em all floating along, and the river'll be full and they won't know what struck em. The Lawd's gonna have his day.

They'll be a war. But it won't be no more wars like the World War. It won't bother me and you. Won't really be no war. It'll be the wicked killing the wicked! The war like the World War'll never be again. They fooled now. They building navies and buying guns. But don't you worry, it'll be just the wicked killing out the wicked. It's coming; God's time is coming and it's coming soon!

I'm lonely tonight. Damn lonely! This business of mine makes you like that sooner or later. It's a tough racket and it's got so a girl can hardly make a decent living anymore. Too many girls. There ain't enough business to go around. There was a time when a girl could go out there and pick up a couple of hundred a week. But that was a long time ago. You gotta do some tall hustling to even get by nowadays. The cops are getting so they want almost half you make for protection. I don't mind kicking in with a few dollars now and then but this business of hustling for somebody else is a different story. Of course, there are a lot of cops who will let you off easy if you are willing to do them a little favor when they're off-duty, but most of them can't be trusted. I know a kid who was run in by a cop only last week and he's one of the very guys she's been paying off for the past couple of years. Now she's cooling her hips in jail. The trouble with that guy was that he was sore because he thought she was giving too much money to her pimp instead of to him.

Pimps are just as bad as the cops. I've never seen a lousier lot of bums in my life. I never got an even break from one since the first day I went into the racket. They're all alike. They put you in some cheap two dollar joint or send you out to pound the pavements, then take every dime of your money and think you oughta like it. Once in a while, they go out and buy up a lot of hot clothes and act like they're doing you a favor buying you some beat-up stuff with your own money.

I'll never forget the first pimp I had. His name was Charlie and I met him one night at the restaurant where my aunt had got me a job. I was eighteen then and I lived with my aunt in St. Louis; my old man and old lady had died when I was just a kid. Anyhow, this guy Charlie looked like a good guy. He was a big black boy with a wide smile and a lot of gold teeth that flashed at you every time he opened his mouth. He was a swell dresser too, and free with his money. He gave me a fifty cent tip the first night he came in there. After that, he came by every night for about two weeks. One night he asked me to go out with him. I went, and it wasn't long before I found out what a swell lover he could be. I was a set-up for him after that. When it finally dawned on me what his game was, I had reached the place where it didn't make any difference to me. I was willing to do anything he said. So I left home and went to live with him.

Not so long afterwards, he put me in a two dollar joint. I didn't like it there and told him so, but he always kissed me or petted me and said that after awhile I wouldn't mind at all. When he was nice and made love to me like that, I forgot all about everything else and the only word I knew was "yes!"

I worked there for about seven months and one day one of the girls got drunk and told me to wake up and get wise to myself, that I was only being a sucker for Charlie and that he had four girls working for him in different houses about town. When I asked him about it, he told me to go to hell and mind my own business. Then, when I tried to leave him, he beat me up and gave me a couple of black eyes. After that when I came in at night, he took all my money and told me he'd cut my throat if I tried to hold out on him. He even used to come to see the women that ran the house so he could find out how much I was making. That way he was able to check up on me. Sometimes, though, I got a good customer who slipped me an extra five or ten. I kept this money and hid it until I had enough to go away. Then one day while Charlie was at the club gambling, I got on the train and went to Chicago.

I had never been there before and it was tough learning the ropes at first. But one night I went down to one of those black-and-tan joints on the South Side and got to talking with a girl who was one of the entertainers there and who broke me in right. She offered to introduce me to some of the boys but I told her I was through with pimps and wanted to be on my own. This good resolution didn't last long, though, and after three or four months, I wanted someone of my own in the worst way. It's awfully tough going home to an empty room night after night like that. If Charlie had come along then, I think I would even have gone back to him.

That's when I started drinking. It was the only way I had of passing the time. Night after night, I wandered from one cabaret to another, just drinking or sitting and watching the dancers. It was while I was out on one of those bats that I met Johnny. He was an awfully nice fellow but it didn't take me long to find out that he was in the racket, too. He wore a lot of flashy clothes and spent money like it was water. I was too wise to fall for that gag, though. They all do that at first. Making a flash, they call it. That's just a bait to make a girl fall for them. So, when Johnny pulled this stuff on me, I told him to nix out. I wasn't interested. I liked my new freedom too well. But he must have seen something in my eyes that told him how lonely I was.

Every day, after that, he used to send me flowers, candy and presents. He treated me like I was a lady. Once he sent me a ring and when I had it appraised, the man told me that it was worth two hundred dollars. The next time he came to see me, it happened. I just couldn't hold out on him any longer. He was so nice to me. He was that way for a long time. But I knew it couldn't last—his way of doing things was just a little different that's all. So when he began hinting that he needed money, I told him he could have every cent I made. There wasn't any need for him to kid me. I knew what he wanted and was willing to give it to him. Having money didn't matter to me any longer, anyhow. All I wanted was him, but I soon found out that that wasn't as easy as it sounded. There was too much competition for him. Everywhere we went, the girls I knew, and some I didn't know, were making a play for him, right and left: especially some who made more money than I did.

Johnny was a good-looking brown-skinned boy with dark, wavy hair and eyes that did something to you. He was a nice boy, too. He had been to college and knew how to talk in that smooth easy way, so different from the rest of those roughnecks around Chicago. It wasn't long before I knew he had another girl. Johnny was like that—ambitious—always wanting more than anybody else, and the best of everything at that. I was jealous and started playing around with some of his friends just to make him sore. One day he came home and found one of them there with me. He left that night. There wasn't any quarrel and he didn't beat me. Johnny was like that—always the gentleman. He was the only man I ever had who didn't beat me. He didn't believe in leaving enemies behind him. It was always his policy, he said, to part friends. When he left, he gave me a beautiful ring: a lovely diamond. I've still got it. It's the only thing I've got that's never been in the pawn-shop.

Being without Johnny was worse than I thought it could be. It finally got so bad that I went to him and begged him to come back to me, but it wasn't any use. He had moved in with a little Spanish chick by the name of Consuelo. She worked in a ritzy joint and made a lot of money. If it had been anybody else, maybe I wouldn't have

felt so bad about it but I never did like that little dame, even before I knew she was after him. She used to hang around the cabarets once in a while, acting snooty and showing off her clothes.

When I thought of her with Johnny, I was almost crazy with jealousy. Once I went on a wild spree and didn't go to work for more than a week. When I finally showed up, another girl had taken my job. After that, I didn't try to find work. Instead, I just lay around drinking with a lot of bum friends who came around and sponged on me. When I got broke, none of them would lend me a dime.

One night when I couldn't stand it any longer, I went to the club where Johnny gambled and asked him to give me some money. He told me that his business was taking money, not giving it. That same night I got lousy drunk and waited in Lulu-Mae's place where I was sure he would meet Consuelo after she got off work. When he showed up, I asked him once more if he would come back to me. He only laughed at me and I was so mad that I went half crazy. I opened my pocket-book and pulled out a little gun that I had been carrying around with me. When Johnny saw it, he dived after me and I pulled the trigger. The next minute, he grabbed his stomach and fell forward on his face. That's all I remember except that the cops came and took me away. I didn't care. If I couldn't have Johnny, I wanted to die anyhow.

I told them that I didn't want a lawyer

but they gave me one just the same. He told me a lot of things to say but I wouldn't say anything. He was smart, though, and got the charge reduced from murder to manslaughter. When it was all over, they sent me up for ten years. But I was paroled after doing five of them. Not long afterwards, I came to New York. That was eight years ago.

New York's just about the same as Chicago as far as the racket's concerned, only it's harder to fix the cops here and especially the Health Department M.D.'s who examine you when you're picked up on the streets. I've spent a lot of time on Welfare Island "taking the cure." Even when I'm able to beat a soliciting rap, these doctors slap a positive-label opposite my name and the Health Department won't let me go until I'm O.K. Sometimes, it takes three, four, even six months. In Chicago it was different. All you had to do was get a smart lawyer who knew the ropes or a fixer who could put a few dollars in the right places for you. That way, you could get a negative label whenever you needed it.

I'm getting sick and tired of this life, but what can I do? I don't know any other kind of work and even if I did, where would I find it? Besides, once you get accustomed to seventy-five or a hundred dollars a week, it's pretty hard trying to get by on fifteen or eighteen.

Christ! I never did anything to deserve a life like this. All I did was to fall in love with a man! There is a God, ain't there? I'm not sure there's anything anymore except cheap women and cheating men.

God! I'd give anything to know what'll become of me!

When I first came to New York from Bermuda, I thought rent-parties were disgraceful. I couldn't understand how any self-respecting person could bear them, but when my husband, who was a Pullman porter, ran off and left me with a sixty-dollar-a-month apartment on my hands and no, job I soon learned, like everyone else, to rent my rooms out and throw these Saturday get-togethers.

I had two roomers, a colored boy and a white girl named Leroy and Hazel, who first gave me the idea. They offered to run the parties for me if we'd split fifty-fifty. I had nothing to lose, so that's how we started.

We bought corn liquor by the gallon and sold it for fifty cents a small pitcher. Leroy also ran a poker and black-jack game in the little bedroom off the kitchen. On these two games alone, I've seen him take in as much as twenty-eight dollars in one night. Well, you can see why I didn't want to give it up once we had started. Especially since I could only make six or seven dollars at most as a part-time domestic.

The games paid us both so well, in fact, that we soon made gambling our specialty. Everybody liked it, and our profit was more that way, so our place soon became the hangout of all those party-goers who liked to mix a little gambling with their drinking and dancing.

And with all these young studs with plenty of cash in their pockets out to find a little mischief, we soon learned not to leave things to chance. Instead, Hazel and I would go out and get acquainted with good-looking young fellows sitting alone in the back of gin-mills looking as if they would like a good time but had nobody to take them out. We'd give them our cards and tell them to drop around to the house. Well, wherever there are pretty women you'll soon have a pack of men.

So we taught the girls how to wheedle free drinks and food out of the men. If they got them to spend more than usual, we'd give them a little percentage or a nice little present like a pair of stockings or vanity case or something. Most of the time, though, we didn't have to give them a thing. They were all out looking for a little fun, and when they came to our house they could have it for nothing instead of going to the gin-mills where they'd have to pay for their own drinks.

And we rented rooms, sometimes overnight and sometimes for just a little while during the party. I have to admit that, at first, I was a little shocked at the utter boldness of it, but Leroy and Hazel seemed to think nothing of it, so I let it go. Besides, it meant extra money—and extra money was what I needed.

I soon took another hint from Hazel and made even more. I used to notice that Leroy would bring home some of his friends and, after they'd have a few drinks, leave them alone in the room with Hazel. I wasn't sure that what I was thinking was so until Hazel told me herself. It happened one day when

an extra man came along and there was no one to take care of him. Hazel asked me if I would do it. I thought about it for awhile, then made up my mind to do it.

That was the last of day-work for me. I figured that I was a fool to go out and break my back scrubbing floors, washing, ironing, and cooking, when I could earn three day's pay, or more, in fifteen minutes, and when I began to understand how Hazel got all those fine dresses and good-looking furs. From then on, it was strictly a business with me. I decided that if it was as easy as that, it was the life for me.

The landlord's agent had been making sweet speeches to me for a long time and I began to figure out how I could get around paying the rent. Well, I got around it, but that didn't stop me from giving rent parties. Everything I made then was gravy: clean, clear profit for little Bernice. I even broke off with Leroy and Hazel. She began to get jealous and catty, and I think he was holding out on profits from the game. Anyway, we split up and I got an "old man" of my own to help me run the house. When he took things over he even stopped girls from going into the rooms with the men unless we were getting half of what they made, and the men still had to pay for the

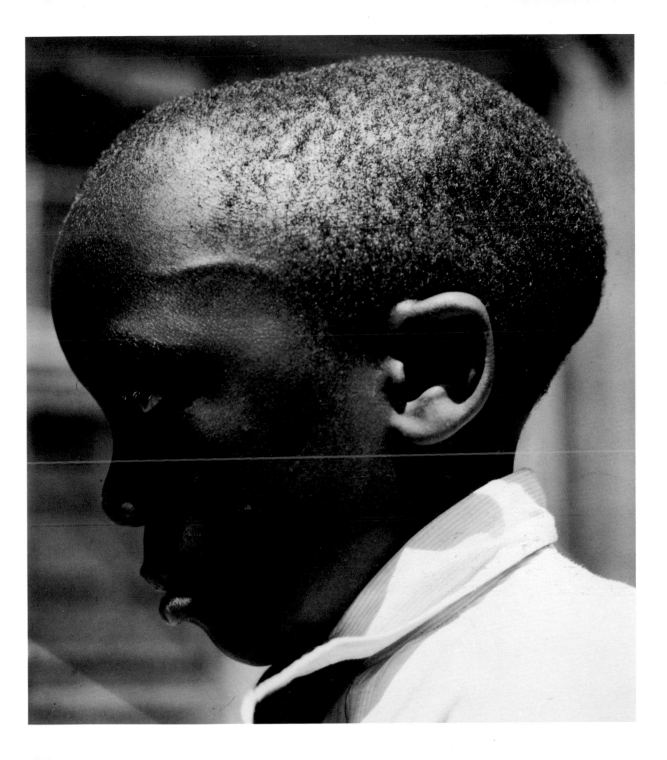

rooms. I've seen some of those girls make enough on Saturday night to buy themselves an entirely new outfit for Sunday, including fur coat. They'd catch some sucker, like a Pullman porter or longshoreman who had been lucky in a game, and have him jim-clean before the night was over. Naturally, I got my cut.

It was a good racket while it lasted, but it's shot to pieces now.

There's a hundred different ways to bring yourself good luck or money or to put the jinx on somebody you don't like. All you have to do is cross the palm of the doctor.

Got an ache in your joints? If you have, boil a few mullen leaves in a pan of water and drink a cup before meals.

Your kidneys bother you? Don't let em. Boil a couple teaspoons of cream of tartar and flaxseed in a pint of water and drink it. You'll feel like a different person.

Ever have trouble renting rooms or your luck go back on you? Put a handful of rice in a bag with some sycamore bark, boil and strain it then sprinkle the contents on both sides of the door-sill.

If your husband or wife ain't treatin you right, feedin you cold supper or staying out nights, buy a handful of tiny red candles, smear them with maple syrup or honey, write the person's name on a piece of brown paper greased with a month old ham-skin and burn the candles under the bed. That'll fix up everything fine.

If your boyfriend or girlfriend leaves you, take one of their old shoes, sprinkle a little "bring em back dust" on the soles, point one to the North and the other to the South. They'll be back in a week unless somebody done used a stronger conjure than you.

If somebody you like act kinda cool get the egg of a frizzly chicken, boil it in spring water, take it out of the shell and eat up the yolk with a lump of sugar, starch and Jimson weed; put it in a bag and hide it in his clothes and he'll wind up being yo slave.

My mother had . . . . sisters, and they all lived in Brooklyn.

A family came up from the South and moved next door to my Aunt Lucy. They seemed like nice folks and were neighborly and quiet. One day the woman from next door—I've forgot her name—came rushing in to my Aunt Lucy. She told her that she had been conjured. Aunt Lucy just laughed and said there wasn't any such thing as conjuring.

Then about a week later, the woman fell sick in bed. Aunt Lucy went to see her, and she told her again that she had been conjured. Aunt Lucy still didn't put any stock in it, and the woman didn't say much to her about it after that. But she kept getting worse. It took her a long time to have a doctor because she kept saying that it wouldn't do any good since she had been conjured. But after the doctor started coming, she didn't seem to get any better. Then, one time when my Aunt Lucy went to see her, she told Aunt Lucy to look under the back steps when she left to go home. Just to keep her quiet, Aunt Lucy told her alright. And do you know that Aunt Lucy found a little bag like tobacco comes in under the steps. It was full of something. Aunt Lucy didn't open it to see what it was because she said she didn't want no part of the mess. She took the bag to the woman. When she showed it to her, she started screaming and carrying on and told Aunt Lucy to take the bag in the kitchen

and put it in the stove and burn it. Aunt Lucy did, but she always said she thought it was foolish. When Aunt Lucy got ready to go home, the woman told her to look on her kitchen window and she'd find some little balls—like berries of the waxberry bush on the window sill. Sure enough, Aunt Lucy did find them, but she always said that the woman next-door had them put there.

The woman started to get better after Aunt Lucy burned that little bag. She swore that she would have died if Aunt Lucy hadn't found that bag and burnt it. Aunt Lucy asked her how she knew it was there, and the woman said that she had a feeling. Course I don't believe it myself, I guess. But it did seem funny that that bag was right where she said. It looked kind of funny, too, when she started getting well after the bag was burnt. But Aunt Lucy said that she just happened to take a turn for the better right long through there, and after all, she did have a doctor.

In 1936 a group of photographers at the Photo League in New York formed a production unit which they called the Feature Group. Some months later Michael Carter, a black writer, came to us with a plan for the making of a document on Harlem. Our work of some three years resulted in a book which was never published. A number of photographs made by me during the years 1932-1936 were included in that work of the Feature Group. In 1940 Max Yavno, Michael Carter and I began another project: The Most Crowded Block. The Second World War overtook us and it was not completed.

In the listing below photographs included in The Feature Group project are indicated by FG. The Most Crowded Block photographs are indicated by MCB. Information about specific photographs is given when I have it. Records kept were incomplete, casual and, alas, even these are mostly gone.

Michaela Murphy made the prints for the reproductions in this book from negatives George Eastman House generously permitted us to use.

Notes on Interviews
by Ann Banks

A Clyde "Kingfish" Smith was one of a group of New York City street vendors interviewed by Marion Charles Hatch and Herbert Halpert in 1939.

B The children's games, rhymes and taunts collected on the streets of Harlem by Ralph Ellison were to have been included in a Federal Writers' Project anthology of children's lore called *Chase the White Horse.* The book was never published.

C The Harlem showgirl who talked to Vivian Morris in 1939 was determined to rise to the top in the one area of the one profession where she had seen black people succeed: show business.

D Jim Barber's strong anti-white sentiments were widely shared in Harlem when he was interviewed by Ralph Ellison in 1939. The white merchants of 125th Street—among them the furniture store owner Barber mentioned—were particularly resented because they refused to hire blacks for any but the most menial jobs. Black responses to this discrimination ranged from boycotts ("Don't Buy Where You Can't Work") to the 1935 riot which left millions of dollars of property damage.

E In May, 1939, at Eddie's Bar in St. Nicholas Avenue a railroad porter just off work told Ralph Ellison of his mixed feelings about New York. It was a theme that absorbed Ellison: and he later hoped to document the changes in the black experience when millions of blacks moved from southern farms to northern cities in the early 20th century. Ellison included the porter's repeated refrain in his novel *Invisible Man:* "Don't let this Harlem git you. I'm in New York, but New York ain't in me, understand what I mean? Don't git corrupted."

F According to background notes, the subject of this interview was "an elderly Negro man, born in Virginia." He expressed his apocalyptic visions and class antagonisms to Ralph Ellison in June of 1939 in a city park in Harlem.

G This Harlem prostitute told Frank Byrd her life story in a Lenox Avenue bar called Red's Joint. "I used to drink with a few people who introduced me to her," Byrd recalled later. "She didn't make any bones about her profession and I talked to her several times. We would drink whatever was available, usually corn whiskey or sometimes gin when we could get it."

H The rent parties described in this story flourished in Harlem in the 1920s, a response to the high rents and low wages blacks faced when they arrived in New York City. Around the time the rent was due, neighbors were invited to a get-together with music, food and corn liquor and charged an entrance fee of fifteen cents or a quarter. Frank Byrd collected this reminiscence in 1938.

I "Sagwa," as he was known, was a West Indian conjure man practicing his trade in Harlem. He was interviewed in 1938 by Dorothy West.